The Welcome Table

MARY BURRITT CHRISTIANSEN
POETRY SERIES
V. B. PRICE, SERIES EDITOR

Also available in the
University of New Mexico Press
Mary Burritt Christiansen Poetry Series:

Poets of the Non-Existent City:
Los Angeles in the McCarthy Era
edited by Estelle Gershgoren Novak

Selected Poems of Gabriela Mistral
edited by Ursula K. Le Guin

Deeply Dug In by R. L. Barth

Amulet Songs: Poems Selected and New by Lucile Adler

In Company: An Anthology of New Mexico Poets After 1960
edited by Lee Bartlett, V. B. Price,
and Dianne Edenfield Edwards

Tiempos Lejanos: Poetic Images from the Past
by Nasario García

Refuge of Whirling Light by Mary Beath

The River Is Wide/El río es ancho: Twenty Mexican Poets,
a Bilingual Anthology
edited and translated by Marlon L. Fick

A Scar Upon Our Voice by Robin Coffee

CrashBoomLove: A Novel in Verse by Juan Felipe Herrera

In a Dybbuk's Raincoat:
Collected Poems by Bert Meyers

Rebirth of Wonder: Poems of the Common Life
by David M. Johnson

Broken and Reset: Selected Poems, 1966 to 2006 by V. B. Price

The Curvature of the Earth
by Gene Frumkin and Alvaro Cardona-Hine

Derivative of the Moving Image by Jennifer Bartlett

Map of the Lost by Miriam Sagan

¿de Veras?: Young Voices from the
National Hispanic Cultural Center
edited by Mikaela Jae Renz
and Shelle VanEtten-Luaces

A Bigger Boat:
The Unlikely Success of the Albuquerque Poetry Slam Scene
edited by Susan McAllister, Don McIver,
Mikaela Renz, and Daniel Solis

A Poetry of Remembrance by Levi Romero

THE WELCOME TABLE

Jay Udall

⌘   ⌘

⌘

*To Katie
in friendship*

UNIVERSITY OF NEW MEXICO PRESS ⌘ ALBUQUERQUE

© 2009 by the University of New Mexico Press
All rights reserved. Published 2009
Printed in the United States of America
14 13 12 11 10 09   1 2 3 4 5 6

Library of Congress Cataloging-in-Publication Data
Udall, Jay, 1959–
The welcome table / Jay Udall.
    p. cm. — (Mary Burritt Christiansen poetry series)
ISBN 978-0-8263-4661-2 (hardcover : alk. paper)
I. Title.
PS3621.D35W45 2009
811'.6—dc22
                2008042270

Designed and typeset by Mina Yamashita
Composed in Arno Pro, a typeface designed
by Robert Slimbach for Adobe.
Printed by IBT Global on 55# Bulking Cream

To my teachers, students, friends

4 sections

Contents

Foreword by V. B. Price / xiii
Acknowledgments / xvii

PART ONE: ANOTHER ANATOMY

    The Cicadas / 3
    The Myth of the Body / 4
    Pilgrimage / 5
    Another Anatomy / 6
    Bee Prophecy / 7
    We Sing to the Lion / 8
    To Weeds / 9
    Eyes / 10
    Mouth to Mouth / 11
    Sacred Datura / 12
    The Mule / 13
    Dog on a Ten-Foot Chain / 14
    Talking with My Hands / 15
    The Donkey / 16
    Again / 17
    Feast / 18
    How I Love the Lion / 19
    The Absolution of the Bee / 20
    Passenger / 21

Part Two: **INTRODUCTION TO THEOLOGY**

    Introduction to Theology / 25
    The Tiger / 26
    There / 28
    Listening In / 29
    Dangling / 30
    The House Detective / 32
    Theophany / 33
    My Mother Cutting Vegetables / 34
    Driven / 36
    At the Banquet of the Dead / 37

Part Three: **THE WELCOME TABLE**

    In the Living Room / 41
    The Wide Door / 42
    A Visitor / 44
    Poem with Father and Lions / 45
    Gloves / 47
    The Seduction / 48
    Hummingbird in the Skylight / 49
    The Night Porch / 51
    Going Down Singing / 53
    Tree Blessing / 54
    Kinship / 55
    Tree Brain / 56
    The Jar: A Sequel / 57
    The Welcome Table / 58
    Tracking William Stafford / 61
    Sleeping with Animals / 62
    Coming and Going / 64

Part Four: **GIVING BLOOD**

    Between Poems / 69
    Prison Poetry / 70
    Neighbor / 71
    Of Unity and Wholeness / 72
    Giving Blood / 74
    Albuquerque / 75
    Sidewalk / 76
    American Marathon / 77
    The Torturer's Hands / 78
    The Caskets / 79
    Many Kingdoms / 80
    Where the Crickets Found Me / 81
    The Great Secret / 82
    A Peace / 84
    Depending / 85
    I Walk to Get Things Moving / 86
    Improvisation in a Changing Key / 87
    Moving / 88

Foreword

Everyone leaves stories behind, and the past is made up of those leavings. The stories are not the same as what actually happened. They might seem the same, but they are merely descriptions, loaded with meaning of their own. The meaning is what matters. It's what makes poetry and the inner history of life in the world. Much as Teilhard de Chardin saw the most personal as the most universal, Jay Udall's exploration of the meanings of the unique personal culture in each of us is so unvarnished, so idiosyncratic and candid, that the poems in *The Welcome Table* feel as if they are the grounding for metaphysical experience that can only be gained in the context of individual lives.

There is a fugue-like quality to Udall's images and evocations as they flow through the poems of this book. Udall gives readers poems within poems, dreams within dreams, the fragrances of the lives within his life, the bewilderments of his younger self snagged within the solitudes of being an adult never old enough to want to outgrow who he has been all his life. Childhood reflections of death and terror are mirrored in the observations of his own daughter who says, "God is eating us up!" *The Welcome Table* explores awakening to one's solitary life that is more than the sum of its history and to one's long, rich responsibility to others in a mysterious world that is at once magnificent, nonsensical, and ruthlessly logical.

These beautifully crafted poems use private memory as the stage upon which to build community with the reader. The poems are less about memoir, I think, than the consciousness we all share as we experience the irreplaceable realities of our encounters with the world as it is, in all its strange glory and harsh disappointment. The human species, Udall shows us, is one life after another, one death after another, dead loves that never die in us until we die, lives lost to themselves in the world's endless meal of the living, hungering for meaning, for a sense of why it was such a revelation to sense as a child that "God was the terror, God the calm." These poems carry me along in the sharp truth of their emotional vision, the entangled darkness and optimism of their philosophical doubt, their quizzing of the infinite, and in the fullness of their humanity. These are the poems of a whole person who never detached from the ideal of fully integrating into himself all his days as he lived them.

The book is organized into four parts: Another Anatomy, Introduction to Theology, The Welcome Table, and Giving Blood. Each part has echoes of the others and all build to a heightened sense of empathy and inwardness directed toward the lost life of childhood, the bodies and lives of other creatures, the pains and courage of the excluded, and the duties we have, giving life's blood and tears, to the way the world actually is.

The title poem of *The Welcome Table* begins with an epigraph from a traditional gospel song: "All God's children gonna sit together . . . / Gonna sit at the welcome table / One of these days." Udall gathers his life around him, taking the essence of that inclusive vision and writes: "The world poured in through your eyes / through your soft tunnels avid mouths. . . . / the silence ringing welcome welcome / before this light in my head goes out / welcome before my last atoms scatter / into cockroach and honeysuckle into / dirt and river welcome petal speck drop / branching dendrite arcing spark / welcome ever after."

Udall's imagination is in solidarity with other forms of life. It is more than sympathy. This solidarity can't help but feel what it's like for a mouse to be caught by a hawk, "the sharp beak / piercing soft neck, / and the warm, salt-sweet blood / of a mouse swept up / from summer's easy field, / shuddering, gasping / ... the dimming cold / spreading in slow waves / toward the heart."

The poet's solidarity is expansive. During a sleepless night, "trying to breathe, / to live between the gear teeth / of an engine devouring earth and blood," he heard "tiny keys opening / night's numberless doors." Later in his garden, in a pile of rocks, he found "in a crevice between two stones . . . / a single cricket, small and brownish-black. / Carefully, carefully, I put the stone back."

Jay Udall's life as a poet has won him many honors, and he has seen his work published in publications large and small. Like most writers, he's held other jobs, including working for many years as the office manager and legal aide for the Navajo Uranium Miners Fund in Santa Fe, New Mexico. He currently teaches writing at the University of Nevada, Reno, and has taught at numerous other colleges and universities, including in the creative writing program at the University of New Mexico. What a catalytic and inspiring experience it must be for students to work with a poet possessing the openness, depth, imagination, and precision of Jay Udall.

—V. B. Price
Albuquerque, New Mexico

Acknowledgments

The following poems first appeared in these publications:

"Introduction to Theology," "The Cicadas," "Pilgrimage," "Another Anatomy," "To Weeds," "The Mule," "We Sing to the Lion," "Coming and Going," "Giving Blood," "The Great Secret," "Whereced the Crickets Found Me," and "Depending" in the chapbook *Another Anatomy* (Finishing Line Press, 2007)

"There" in *Natural Bridge*

"Dangling" in *Coe Review*

"The House Detective" in *Phantasmagoria*

"The Myth of the Body" in *Caesura*

"Eyes" and "The Donkey" in *Manzanita Quarterly*

"Sacred Datura" in *Sage Trail*

"Dog on a Ten-Foot Chain" in *Revolve*

"Again" in *Blessed Pests of the Beloved West* (anthology, Native West Press, 2003)

"The Absolution of the Bee" in *The Albuquerque Tribune*

"Tree Blessing" and "Neighbor" in *Central Avenue*

"In the Living Room" in *The Pedestal*

"The Wide Door" in *Spoon River Poetry Review*

"A Visitor" in *Midwest Quarterly*

"Poem with Father and Lions" and "Many Kingdoms" in *The Dirty Napkin*

"Gloves" and "Hummingbird in the Skylight" in *Tar River Poetry*

"The Seduction" in *White Pelican Review*

"Tracking William Stafford" in *Louisville Review*

"Prison Poetry" in *The Kerf*

"Of Unity and Wholeness" in *Rattle*

"American Marathon" in *Cutthroat: A Journal of the Arts*

"The Torturer's Hands" in *Dos Passos Review*

Part One

ANOTHER ANATOMY

⌘   ⌘
⌘

The Cicadas

The ground opens—
clean holes in hard earth—
and silent brown shells
crawl for the nearest branches
to leave themselves,
splitting down the middle,
climbing out to hang dry
with staring orange eyes,
ghostly bodies slowly going
black, touched with fine strokes
of orange on head and back.
Now they own the air,
bursting from branches
as we pass, rasping,
screeching, scratching
the skin of our faces
and limbs, snagging our hair,
while somewhere unseen
a great hovering machine
ratchets higher and higher,
rising to a scream.
The years break open—
we climb out, feel for
any touch of before—
air, earth, skin: a door.

The Myth of the Body

When the white paint cracked, curling
in ragged strips off the fence, I saw
the old flesh of trees underneath,
gray fiber loosening, spreading
to hummingbird light and air.
Two sticks in the grass became snakes.
A face in a boulder,
another in a cloud.
I saw my mother's arms,
so thin and gray, stiffening
on their final sheet—a doe
bounding past the window.
How the body loves to dream
beyond itself, as if blood
conceived spirit, as if night
and dust and marrow.

Pilgrimage

I'm tired of monotheism.
I, for one, for many, prefer the cockroach
emerging from the ivy, reading
the night with quivering antennae,
the fat rattlesnake that turned me back
out of the canyon's rocky throat,
presences in a hallway of willows.
Yesterday we scrubbed slippery, clayish mud
from the season's first potatoes, their irregular
roundnesses all the psalms my palms ever wanted.
I traveled more than half a life
to get here—just don't ask me how.
I left the cat sleeping beneath the morning table
and walked out along the dry rain ditch that runs
behind neighborhoods stunned by heat, past grass banks
burnt the color of hay, faltering cinder-block walls,
waves of orange trumpet and grape vines
breaking over fences, a tree house rotting
in the green branches of a mulberry, its tenant
having long since descended.
I walk toward mountains I will not reach,
toward my death, but the mourning doves
and sumacs walk their own stories.
One minute I'm alone, and the next
belongs to leaves and ghosts. How many voices
have frequented that catalpa? Who is wandering
my blood? I build a shrine in my feet
for worlds to come through. I let the wind
arrange the windows.

Another Anatomy

Suppose our blood remembers
warming in reptilian sun
on stones beside a droning river,
and our skin remembers
sleeping inside mouse fur
in a house of earth.
Suppose this body knows
the sharp beak
piercing soft neck,
and the warm, salt-sweet blood
of a mouse swept up
from summer's easy field,
shuddering, gasping
as the river tears
open to the light,
the dimming cold
spreading in slow waves
toward the heart.

BEE PROPHECY

Walking through summer fir and aspen
thinking of something I'll never remember

lost in some other life entering
a small meadow white and yellow

I stepped into a haze of bees
that parted easily as air

wings and fur brushing my skin
as I went in deeper deeper

afraid to stop or turn back
unable to see the end

barely breathing the swarming
filling my mouth with fuzzed speech

I say what I can it was leaf
lungs and sky a shining

hive we live inside

We Sing to the Lion
for Gerald Stern

I wake with my head in his mouth.
He tames us with roaring,
makes us wild with his singing,
his friendship, his naps by the window,
growling if we disturb his rest.
Where are we going next?
He doesn't know—or refuses to say,
though sometimes a sudden field blossoms
for the dancing of our hooves and feet and paws.
On payday he hands us envelopes
stuffed with galaxies, mud.
A Bactrian camel, a golden lion tamarin monkey,
a capybara—someone is always arriving
and departing on the slow river.
When we call home, a familiar voice says
the line's been disconnected, then hangs up.
We become family,
cleaning each other's bones with our teeth
and singing, singing to the lion
as we stare down his throat.

To Weeds
to Stanley Kunitz, in memoriam

Rising through cracks, through seams
between asphalt, concrete, thoughts,
invading pure beds, taking vacant lots
with your coarse leaves, prickling stalks, cursed
blossoms, roots of wire, Hydra's heads
multiplying in the mothering dark;
rising with wolf spiders, black mamba snakes,
three-armed babies, lava, earthquakes—
wild messengers, emissaries of chaos,
rise through my clocks, names, deaths, eyes.

EYES

Across the desert's dark body
scraps of mica scatter sparks of moonlight—
millions of mirrors, stars, eyes.
Lying beside you, your body incandescent
in sleep, I'm seen, I see—
eyes in fingertips and skin,
in hair, genitals, tongues,
in the green silence of leaves
outside our window, eyes
in the hollow shell of a beetle
found in a disregarded field,
in the faces of childhood friends
returning unbidden, asking for my hand,
in the motionless cane of an old man
murdered by soldiers while crossing a bridge.
Eyes in purple verbena beside the road.

Mouth to Mouth

Swimming up from nowhere,
the mulberry leaves wound me—
a sudden well between
the avocado's skin
and its pale green softness,
unwalled room
where the inner curve
of an artichoke leaf
meets a ridge of teeth.
Who put the sky right here,
between my nose and chin?
It's only because it knows it will
die that it wants to eat you
whole, like a slice of bread.
But you rise and rise again
and I'm swallowed and swallowed
by the mimosa and the hummingbird
resting in its branches.
When death drinks me, it will taste
volcanoes, harmonicas, cucumbers, cheetahs,
layered leaves taking the sun.
It will wonder where I've gone.

SACRED DATURA
for Kate Krasin

Diaphanous five-clawed star
rising from dust and dog shit
fluted funnel creamy mouth
swallowing night into deep
green going underground
silent trumpet playing
to each passing ear
enter here my
house of
dreams

The Mule

Quietly the mule hauls its load.
Rocking side to side up the trail,
I gaze into distances: back down
across the switchbacks we've climbed,
toward the river, a green blur
disappearing between canyon walls;
or up ahead, through blue haze, where the far
ridgeline seems to rise as we approach,
receding into sky. I begin dreaming
and my mule disappears
for a few minutes or many days
—until he snorts or suddenly stops,
as if to think of these endless hills,
of cool water, food and rest.
When I finally lie down to sleep
on difficult ground, under jumbled stars,
the mule lies down beside me.
Some nights I forget who I might be
and sunlight finds my mule eyes,
warms my long ears and flanks.
Then I remember everything.

Dog on a Ten-Foot Chain

He knows how to wait
watching people pass
in light and dark through
the years watching
the same fragment of sky
the same pine tree
the same scrap of yard
dirt packed smooth and hard
beneath his paws
an island of the present
circling the sun
through stock-market fluctuations
weddings elections wars
with hollow bones
the days pour through
forgetting what he is
what he's waiting for
as he watches
from a deepening cave
the people passing
in light and dark
the same fragment of sky
same pine tree
same scrap of yard
dirt packed smooth and hard
beneath his paws

Talking with My Hands

Dangling from the left rim of the tub
resting on my right thigh in warm water
suddenly you frighten me

I hold you up to read this text
of crazed flesh, lines deeper
more plentiful than I recall
now you're reading me

I call you as a master calls
his dogs back into the house
but you're not mine, you say
you're passengers arriving
from places that no longer exist
except in your arriving

And now you claim you're part paw
part fin, flipper, talon, feeler, claw
a host of presences
ten blind seers telling the world
as worms tell the earth

And who am I to doubt you
the way you sometimes linger
when touching bark or stone or skin
as if reading a lost letter
from some stranger, kin

The Donkey

After he accepts our offering
of carrots, the donkey turns sideways,
leans in, pressing against the wire fence—
bony shoulder, broad middle, flank, black
hair pushing through the gray metal grid,
inviting our hands. Rachel, two years old, laughs
at his insistence, at her own pleasure in touching
the coarse, dusty coat, the way he gently
snorts and paws the ground in response.
His breath is hot on our palms, his fur
even hotter, a fierce concentration of sun,
his white muzzle surprisingly smooth
above the wiry whiskers that seem
to loiter around the mouth and nose.
Large, runny nostrils narrow into a dark interior.
Large brown eyes, ringed in white, open and close
in a dreamy rhythm with our stroking hands,
our bodies remembering, teaching us
how to speak through the fence.

Again

A speck traverses the curve
of a circular white world—
the tiniest spider I've ever seen
crawling inside yesterday's coffee cup.
I turn the cup over, rap the side
against my open palm to help him out—
too hard. Too hard. I've killed
again.

Feast

How many times have I washed
these same spoons, forks and knives
while thinking of other things,
liking their shapes, how they take and hold
the water's heat, then let it go.
Glasses, cups, bowls, plates
break, vanish, but these remain,
shining surfaces worn to a dull glow
like sun through smoked glass,
handles rubbed smooth by passing hands.
Which of these knives did my mother use
the last time she ever came to dinner?
Chickens, pigs, cows, fish stream into red.
A fork from my childhood,
splayed tines waiting to feed.

How I Love the Lion

Gently, gently I stroke his brow
and back across his radiating mane
tawny gold, smoldering orange, burnt umber
he wanders far inside
luxuriant as he dozes in his cage
though his legs twitch, eyelids flutter
like heat lightning on the horizon
though a faint moan rises
hidden claws and teeth growing
with my fear he knows I'm near
though half of me has run he returns
my hand to my wrist, I touch
his massive shoulder, bone
clothed in sinew and savanna
soft fur, soft fingers, sun warm
on his ribs I rest my palm
pulse of another sun
all my colors roaring

The Absolution of the Bee

The bee enters the magenta mouth
burrowing into the bright yellow petals
curled and waiting in a circle at the bottom
of the cholla blossom each finger of sun
stroking her in turn each touch leaving
the finest golden dust unseen the red coal
breathing redder inside the striped furred shell
as she goes and goes into that goodness
as if dragged drugged stumbling almost
rolling on her back like a dog in the grass
not knowing this cannot she cannot last
or so we suppose

So let us be forgiven if
in certain moments we forget the shadow
of our urgent pleasure the dark companion
of this frenzied going in and in as if to dissolve
in unbounded sweetness forever
the best death we can imagine
then coming back through senses stunned alive
to gather what we can with prodigious tongues and six
legs gathering from belly back flanks and head
the sweet gold that feeds our kind of making
O let us be forgiven if sometimes we rise
and swing away on a string of air

Passenger

I pull my body up
out of sleep, show my eyes the light,
explain mourning doves to my ears,
rose petals to my fingertips.
I feed it, groom it, dress it,
preparing it for work,
but it lags, lingers over the memory
of Suzanne's nipples last night,
the thinning thread of a dream.
Fears the knife on the counter.
Into the canyons of commerce,
into the desert of plenty
I drive my body where I need to go,
while these eyes keep seeking savannas,
these feet want only to wander,
nose longs for anything real, ears listen for a spring.
The scar on my right forearm,
shaped like a crescent moon,
rises from my seventh year,
the cool of a barn in early summer,
a gleaming piece of sheet metal
leaning against large gold steps of hay.
By windows that don't open,
my body sits obediently,
a lion filling with fire,

someone sobbing,
a house in night.
I bring it home,
past other bodies flowing home,
to touch the bodies it knows
and is known by, in ecstasy,
in anger, in sorrow, in silence
I lay it down, I surrender,
I'm carried away.

Part Two

INTRODUCTION TO THEOLOGY

⌘ ⌘

⌘

Introduction to Theology

The pastor wore olive-green fisherman's waders
under his black robe at the baptism.
I wore my swimming suit and a white robe
with lead weights in the hem so my body
would stay hidden when I stepped down
into the cold water of the glass-fronted font.
I didn't know we were hiding from God.
Masturbating, I always felt so alone, unholy.
No one told me God was in my cock,
in the hand that stroked my cock,
in the warm sperm that clung to my hand.
I don't know when or where my fear began—
it must have come with me into the world.
I stood in a crib with light overtaking the room,
crying, no one coming, only light, no one.
I cried until the light took me in its arms.
God was the terror, God the calm.

The Tiger

I was five, riding with my favorite stuffed tiger
and the luggage in the back of our '56 Chevy
wagon, behind my five siblings, someone's
friend, our mother—all jammed in together
for the bickering miles, the merciless hours.
Big brother Tom, sixteen and the ink still drying
on the license in his wallet, was driving us
across the Promised Land on Route 66,
two lanes of insane speed featuring
frequent near-misses of head-on collisions,
restless passers enjoying the sweet
mobility of postwar boom.
None of us believed in seat belts.
Our big-shot father would fly over all
this misery and danger to meet us
fresh in Santa Fe, our final destination.
I was the youngest, which meant my status
vacillated wildly between cat's meow
and whipping boy. Mostly I tried to keep
a low profile with my tiger and comic books
in our nest of blankets among the baggage.
In a Tennessee campground some of those
suitcases rolled down a hill into a stagnant
river, the home of vulture-sized mosquitoes
who came in the dark to needle us through
our sleeping bags, chasing us to fitful,
cursing sleep in the car. In Arkansas
we discovered a great open cesspool
behind a service station and took turns

flushing the toilet inside while the rest
watched the pond of piss and shit bubble.
Then, somewhere in Oklahoma, I think,
we passed an awful crash, paramedics
helping a man whose right arm seemed
to hang from his body by a string.
Just outside of Santa Fe our car caught fire.
We watched from a safe hill as livid flames
incinerated our summer dreams, a giant tree
of gray-black smoke blossoming higher and
higher in the blue, blue desert sky. Too late
a Good Samaritan, a scrawny man with thick
glasses, stopped to help, spraying a thin stream
of foam from his miniature extinguisher at the
conflagration as he circled the burning metal
shell and his wife screamed, "Harold, be careful!
Don't use it all up!" The place where I'd been
sitting melted, along with nearly everything else,
before the firemen arrived. Yet afterward
someone handed me my tiger. His orange fur
singed around the edges, his right ear
charred black, he reeked of smoke,
but I knew right then I would keep him.
He seemed more precious than before,
worthy of admiration and respect, even wonder
and awe. If you knew how, you could go into the fire
and come out the other side.

THERE

for William Meredith, in memoriam

Tired and late we finally pulled off,
stopped at the first place we found,
a forgotten mom-and-pop motel
off by itself beneath some old trees,
with a faded fern-green wing chair
and musty bedsheets waiting inside.
It was Ohio—or maybe Illinois,
and I was a boy nine or ten,
dreaming my way west in the dark
with my father and our poet friend.

Morning said where we were,
my eyes still baffled by sleep and travel,
another long day's drive yawning ahead,
and as we pulled away, you turned
to me and casually said, "If we hadn't stopped
last night, that place might not have been there."

Listening In

Never talk about your brother on the phone, Mom says
they've tapped it because he's deserted the army
they want to put him in jail for refusing to kill
thank you J. Edgar Hoover and Richard M. Nixon
ten years old cousin Joe and I take turns
listening to that new hollow sound
in the receiver, that ghostly clicking, ticking
"We know you're there," we say
"Shit! Fuck!" then hang up quick
while Mom drives around day and night
smoking Silva Thins, watching the rearview mirror
stopping at random phone booths to call Scott
in Santa Fe, plan his escape to Canada
thank you Robert McNamara for your thick
fog of war, your mathematics of death
does my brother count since he didn't die
did you think it would end it would end it would
the prophet you spoke: there will always be wars
but soon you'll rest in peace, close your eyes
my brother is calling, talking through years
of Thorazine, Haldol, Clozaril, I close my eyes
try to follow his splintering thoughts
his voice arriving across floorless space
sometimes I even think I know where we are

Dangling

I'm eleven, dangling sixty feet above
large, gray, jagged boulders,
tied to the end of a thin piece of rope.

My brother, Denis, has often wished me dead,
but the fear on his face a minute ago
was real—as suddenly everything

has become: this rope, those rocks,
the cloudless early summer sky,
olive-green Potomac flowing

slowly past, this moment, my life.
He said he'd teach me rock climbing,
but the truth is, he doesn't know shit.

Now he's gone for help, tied the other end
to a small tree below, left me here
alone, far from any house or road.

If I fall, no one will see me or hear
my cry—not my mother, not even my dog,
who in her excitement has abandoned me

to follow Denis with the other dogs.
Years plunge. Friends plummet past
while I'm looking the other way.

I wake, wet with cold sweat,
in stranger's skin, falling through
a mattress, finding no bottom.

I wake again to discover that my mother
has fallen out of the world.
I watch us burn our only house

and murder each other's children.
I look down, ride this breath, feel the curve
and stretch of blue, my brother running,

the men fishing the spillway a half mile upstream,
the river arriving and sliding away,
a voice asking, *How long can this last?*

The House Detective

Sometimes when they would leave and I had the house
alone, I'd become a stranger in those halls and rooms—
an intruder, detective, thief. In a trance of adrenaline
and guilt, I'd begin searching through their closets
and drawers, through every pocket of every shirt, jacket,
dress and purse. I didn't know what I was looking for
among the lipstick cases, the loose change, matchbooks,
scraps of paper with scribbled numbers and names,
those ordinary objects I handled as if they held some
secret significance, though once I found a letter that
came close: from mother to father, revealing how
she couldn't take any more and was ready to leave.
I couldn't have guessed the depth of that unhappiness
looming beneath the surface of our common life,
so little did I know them, so little did they show.
That day I realized how much I lived alone.
Later, I might have told myself I was seeking only
the money that bought sodas and cigarettes,
but even then I think I knew there was something
more that kept me sifting their belongings, perhaps
the vague hope that in some pocket or drawer,
hidden among the hairpins and cuff links, I might
at last come upon their true names.

Theophany

When God came to save and damn me
I was stoned on homegrown, fourteen.
His disciples found us outside a pizza joint,
beside caged birds in a skyless mall,
handed us pamphlets, spoke in kind voices.
When they turned away to find others to save,
Gary and Joe cackled, threw their tracts
in the trash. I laughed, too, but secretly
slipped mine in my back pocket.

Already death had kissed my head
five times—friends, a cousin, a neighbor—
I saw black bleeding into every face.
That night, alone in my closet,
I did as the words said. I kneeled
by my shoes and surrendered
to the Son, waited for what came next,
wanting wings or fire, wanting to shed
my flesh or step through some final door,
ready for anything—but the sudden voice
saying, "You *are* God"

and I fled. My lamp and bed,
the wide night—even the silence
hummed like a blade.

My Mother Cutting Vegetables

It was in her face, in the way she held the knife
and the tomato or celery, whatever it was,
as she stood at the kitchen counter.
I see her white hair, burgundy robe
(was it burgundy?) and insomniac eyes—
morning, I think, I'm eating toast and cereal
at the table, she's already preparing
that night's dinner, maybe guests coming,
always guests so we won't be alone
with each other, ourselves. She doesn't know
I watch, she's just herself, and in her face,
in her tired shoulders and arms, in her hands
the thing she will never say, it is too much,
who would listen, she is too busy planning
the happiness of others, including me. Yet
they come, filling the kitchen, flesh resurrected,
ghostly, mute, they gather by the counter to watch
her slicing carrots as if she's performing
an act of great difficulty and significance—

the father exploded by a stick of faulty dynamite
before she turned five, the brother shredded
by a land mine in southern France, the brother crushed
in his car crossing town, a nephew, friends, children
of friends, her mother, even some of the living:
my mad brother, my father and his women.
She doesn't look up, pretends they're not there.
At eighteen I can feel them in the room,
but it will take me many years to see them.
I'll forget this moment, rise from my chair
and stumble into my life, learning
to rage against her silence.
She will have to die, then I'll return
to my place at the table, she'll stand
again at the counter, cutting vegetables,
and I will finally, finally see.

DRIVEN

Do you remember the perfect neighborhoods
of our youth? The perfect houses that held
perfect lives? The immaculate yards
that sang no pain no passion no pain?
We turned the key and pulled away
from our mothers and fathers, their names
strangled in their throats. We drove
and kept driving, driving acid-fueled circuits
of city and suburb, spiraling in and out
past fields where horses stood lonely
in winter light, past vanishing woods,
the ends of runways, planes lifting over
us into a dream of sky, past the prostitutes
working the headlights on 14th Street,
the sleeping houses of girls whose faces
made us ache, as we haunted our own streets
and lives, an unknown voice crying out
from inside the radio, as we reached
the rim of the world, light breaking
in, making everything new, a moment
passing, passing on, dissolving
like the smoke of our countless cigarettes
into a day that sighed, closed its eyes
and fell in line with all the others,
leaving our scorched eyes still
searching, searching for anything
to make us forget the nothingness
that looked back each time we looked
in the rearview mirror.

At the Banquet of the Dead

I sit beside you again
at a table in a room
without beginning or end.
Everyone is laughing.
I don't recognize the other faces
gathered, though I forget to look
for my grandparents, a cousin
and two childhood friends.
Everyone is laughing, laughing
and then I am, too—
a sound like something breaking
loose, like giving up
and giving away
everything forever.
I have to know,
I have to know
if everyone knows that secret.
Your smile is kind.
It doesn't matter,
I think you say,
it doesn't matter.
Then the laughter falls off
and your voice is lost.

Part Three

THE
WELCOME TABLE

In the Living Room

The sun unasked unpaid spends itself
turning the backyard power lines
to lustrous threads for crows
revises the cottonwood's dying limbs
revealing hundreds of glossy buds
and shows the sequences of mimosa
seeds still suspended in parchment
while stroking pine needles to electric hair
tracing lattice and vine walking through
windows to make the houseplants glow
in green translucence warming the white
cat sprawled in a slanting rectangle
swarming in fibers and cloth in the knots
whorls and waves of the table's grain
in the forms and faces in the pictures
on the walls in the light of other times
in time entering every living room
through eye fur feather skin sending
its gift to the concrete porch and
the corpse of the cockroach
the cat left on the floor

The Wide Door

I close my eyes and see
my dead beside me

The boy who fell or hanged himself
in the tangled ropes of his tree house
speaks of the night I walked home
six years old through watching trees
having risen from the bed beside him
to escape the fearful hours
falling from the grandfather clock
the puppy he dropped
falling from the high balcony
to see if it would fly
in his hands a piece of rope becomes
the belt his father took to his back
teaching him to be good

And here's the man who needed
more than we could give
singing through his large bent nose

his voice reaching
through me toward something
on the other side of air
he strums a red guitar with a gun
his brain open to the sky

My mother carries a worn book
heavy with birthdays and anniversaries
the names of children
inseams waists collars sleeves
she is counting the clouds
and the leaves on the trees
recording their addresses
as she walks pages fly up
catching fire in the air

Hundreds of minuscule fingers
outside on the chamisa
reach to blossom

A Visitor

After the televisions turn off
and then the lights, it creeps back
into town and passes through
each neighborhood like a ghost
looking for something or someone.
You can hear it in the strong arm of wind
that tries your windows and doors,
or in the quiet inside the quiet,
an ancient room hollowed out of the air.
As an offering, leave a glass of water
on your kitchen table overnight
and it will show its endless thirst
by sipping off a drop or two.
The sky will give you back your eyes
if you can bear so much seeing.
You will wake to silent voices
that seem to come from the mountains
or from under the ground. You will hear
yourself say to the dark, *Who's there?*

Poem with Father and Lions

I mop my father's pee from the floor
while the lion rubs against the arms in the trees.

The gentle eyes of that boy
who hit a baseball so far into the woods
we never found it.

Smell of oil sticks to my skin.
Gut-churn, basement-rattle; flame-light
through seams and grate shakes shadows
on the ceiling, walls. Behind the furnace
I hide from him.

His hands: pebbles and sticks,
contours of a vanishing path
leading down through trees thick
toward the river's roar.

I follow a man I don't know
through a hole in a chain fence,
past the names and their years,
the forgotten city,
and come alone to a monument
of diaphanous marble: empty.

We watch the sky arrive and arrive,
so many lions running
inside the sunlight,
through the tunnels within leaves,
through our eyes, hands, so many lions
robed in gold—such soft jaws—
light devouring light.

GLOVES

The first day of real cold
I pull out a jacket I haven't worn
in two years—the one
with the black leather arms,
the black wool torso,
the accordion player sewn in shades
of green, blue and red velvet on the back,
a forgotten version
of myself, a shell, a skin
I slip back into.
Then find in the left pocket
a crumpled pair of Rachel's gloves
from the winter she was two—
the ones I loved, each finger
a different color, purple palms,
twin lorikeets flying
through the desert of cold.
I'd slip her small hand halfway in,
try to line up each wayward digit
with its proper hole,
then pull the glove on
before those fingers moved again—
often two or three times to find the fit.
In my hands now these bright husks,
those hands flown.

The Seduction

Kissed on the lips, in the mouth
by honeysuckle nectar
sucked from the stem of the cup
by the crunch and cold juice
of watermelon deep in summer

Caressed by the same light
that swells the pistil and stamen
of iris and gumweed
by lilac, lavender, sage
by the secrets of the rain

Stripped naked by a snake at my feet
by quarks and dark matter
and the stuttering reach
of starred silence unending
the stem of night flowering
faces gone into ash
voices gone into rain
our bodies burning
your touch like smoke

Hummingbird in the Skylight

The way the hummingbird finally surrendered
when I wrapped her blue-green iridescence
in the pillowcase, her body almost weightless
yet warm, a finger through the cloth.
The way she gave herself over, out of pure
exhaustion, to whatever was coming next,
to me, unlikely savior who savors the flesh
of chickens and cows and fish at the table below.
After the doctors sliced open Suzanne's abdomen
and pulled our daughter from her wet red womb,
I held Rachel with a tenderness that came
from somewhere only my blood remembered,
early April light purring at the window,
sounds of afternoon traffic, fat nurses
treading the hall—all of it helping me
improvise fatherhood. I didn't know I would
slap her face hard when she was three.
So I carry the ladder from garage to dining room
and climb to the bottomless eye, desert sun
magnified in its curve, air brutally hot, frozen
hard above, a place no one could live for long.

So my prodigal father comes to me
with fading eyes asking again for my help.
I give him a bowl of oatmeal, conversation
of current events, while we wait for his letting go.
When I unfold the pillowcase and hold her
up in the open air, she doesn't move
her tiny head, feathers like fish scales,
long black needle of a bill so still
against the field of red and gold flowers,
but her eyes blinking, as if waking,
not yet able to believe her luck.

The Night Porch

The rocking chair rocks empty
on the porch where you sat
only moments ago
                            was it just the wind
rolling in through the trees
breaking against the windows and walls
riding the chair

But now you return
from pissing in the pinyons
or stubbing out a cigar
        a spray of sparks
        a quick galaxy
and turn to look back
through the smoke of night
toward the shimmering city
the familiar silhouettes
of the mountains beyond
with your failing eyes
what do you see

Now you're my father now a stranger
now you carry me on your shoulders
through a tunnel of green leaves and water

now you fly away to walk among the stars
and leave me crying now you're crying in bed
as you kiss the still warm cheek and curl
around the corpse of the woman who
loved you for fifty-seven years now you wake
and reach to find nothing now you say
you want to die now you remember dying
inside a mask dreaming inside another woman
now you're a statue too fragile for touch
now you touch my shoulder as you pass
you crucify and resurrect yourself
again and again

Now you're a stranger now my father
now a doorway to first and last light
now you stand alone looking out
dying with your visions now I kiss
your wet cheek you're a boy
disappearing for your father
dreaming while your horses wander
fields opening inside my eyes now
you're my son my father my son
now I stand alone looking out
now the chair rocks empty

Going Down Singing

Where the arroyo curves into a wall
of crumbling gray granite streaked with green
and the willows follow filling the curve
there's only space for one to pass between
where rocks suffer the obsessive sun
and a coolness flows out of the leaves
as if from a room deep in the secret earth
where I pause in the stillness listening
and sand slowly starts to swallow my feet
as if I could stay for however long it might take
weeks years the rest of my life to be buried alive
sinking ever so gradually watching the wind
improvise with the clouds and branches
beginning to chant going down beyond grief
words leaving my throat at the last learning
to sing as willow rock sand

Tree Blessing

All day I live as if you are not here.
My mind says you have no mind, nobody
home inside, no inside, yet sometimes I feel
a presence pressing against the pane—
and there you are, out some window, as if
waiting for something, beckoning.
What do you want? You say nothing, nothing.

At night I hear you move with the wind—
the sound of someone breathing in the dark.
I lie in bed and listen, and listen, my breath
becoming a prayer, until I know
I have your blessing,
you have what you want.

Kinship

My loneliness is told
by the severed neck of a guitar
at the edge of a parking lot,
by ghostly purple-blue juniper berries
withering in cold dust.
It's a waterfall
frozen in sheer air,
claws growing in from my skin,
a dead man with a bottle of bourbon, one lung
and a carton of Marlboro Lights.
But loneliness taught me the kinship of weeds
and how to receive the cottonwood's reachings.
In flatulent sleeping bags beside the Colorado
we watched for meteors skimming the lucid roof,
slow satellites blinking through summer stars.
I didn't know we were gazing into patterns
that existed only as light
traveling eons to enter our eyes—so much
afterimage: your scowl and laughter,
flask of whiskey tucked inside your belt,
the fierce, stricken intelligence of your eyes.
Lime-green lichen feeds on the flank of a boulder,
some nameless weed spreading
like ice crystals along the path.

TREE BRAIN

A man eats the soft, sweet flesh
of banana: Ecuador
and a galaxy of ghosts.
Who grew this wall?
We're alone: we're never alone.
God became the name of our longing
to rise free of the earth forever,
but the cottonwood of two hemispheres
walks its double spine-stalk into winter.
Unintentional kindness of sun,
bitterness of January—
how can I refuse such love?
Breath, blood and dust of the dead
renewed: a Christmas poinsettia
on a crimson tablecloth,
branching roots reaching through the floor.
Father, I've hauled your tons too long.
I lay you in the ground,
let it carry you awhile, awhile.
Mother, gather the wayward jackets
with my hand. My face is being eaten.
From inside the tangled brown vines
on the fence, a singing of many throats.
The follicles in my scalp do their quiet work.

THE JAR: A SEQUEL
after Wallace Stevens

On a hill in Tennessee
a gray jar filled with night, then
light, rain, snow; froze, thawed, again
and again, until it shattered

quietly on the creeping floor.
Neither bird nor bush seemed to care.
Its sharp edges wore away,
molecules dissolving as the slovenly

weeds and vines covered the shards
burning into dirt, into the place
from which the mind that stood apart
and shaped the jar had come.

The Welcome Table

All God's children gonna sit together ...
Gonna sit at the welcome table
One of these days
—Traditional gospel song

Risen from secret enfoldings,
from earth hum, shudder and echo,
seeing and breathing through the length
of their skins, contracting, pushing forth,
shouldering through the hug-and-give
up into wide air, they spread across wet asphalt,
soaked slack, pale threads of living flesh
offered to shoes, tires, returning sun and birds.

※

As a boy I hid among corpses
until the soldiers had passed.
Only a game, though I always felt
I'd gotten away with something.

Eight years old I called my mother to come
rescue me from a friend's house in the night.
Lying in his room, in the bunk above,
in the throat of the dark,
I could feel him dying of his disease
and somehow knew no one could save him
from his angry blood, translucent skin.

He was alone, and I was alone, and so
was my mother, and so was the night
we drove through toward home.

⌘

In white dresses, white shirts, white pants, white shoes
in hidden rooms they recite the names of the dead
for water and resurrection, calling the long rolls
while there's still time, trying to redeem every death
ever recorded in the history of the planet.

⌘

Who is singing in the voices of the crickets?

Whose face is this,
patched together from fraying maps,
borrowed skin, chickens, phrases?

Breathing, I'm breathed.

⌘

Meanwhile, in heaven, after the joyous reunions,
after reminiscing each instant of living
untold times, after gazing at the pure, perfect
scenery and each other's changeless features
for eternity, they don't want to say it,
to appear ungrateful or hurt anyone's feelings—

it seems so contrary to the whole spirit of the place—
but they're growing nostalgic for time and death.

⌘

The world poured in through your eyes
through your soft tunnels avid mouths
until you became the ghostly string
dancing in earth worm purple ash
arriving in the rain it's you i drink
you i eat in blackberries and meat
you tell my tongue you hear my ears
the silence ringing welcome welcome
before this light in my head goes out
welcome before my last atoms scatter
into cockroach and honeysuckle into
dirt and river welcome petal speck drop
branching dendrite arcing spark
welcome ever after

Tracking William Stafford

1.

While others argued in tight circles
about traditions and individual talents,
you snuck away to some forgotten field
transfigured by last night's snow
to catch the latest conversation
between river, trees and sky.
What you heard led you on
across the trackless expanse
that changed at any step
into talking earth or air,
abandoned Kansas prairie,
the translucent ceiling
of a bottomless lake.
Touch by touch, you followed
the path your words were making,
your faith in a thread too fine
to see, your only destination
the edge of any becoming.

2.

Standing at the end of the last line
of your last poem, written the day you died,
we gaze into a country barely visible
through the flakes swarming the air like gnats.
Your mother's voice, your hand and name
move in and out of a light so fearsome,
it can only be answered by trust.
And the sun comes. It comes.

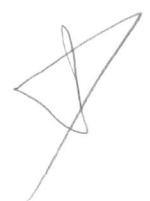

Sleeping with Animals

There was a gray tabby who always curled
around my head, purring loudly by my worried brain,
and a mutt who seemed to sense when I was ill,
the warm pressure of her back against my legs melting
a hardness in me I couldn't let go. Both are gone.
And it felt like an honor, some form of initiation,
when I woke, eleven years old, near dawn
with six new kittens stirring between my legs,
their mother licking birth slime from their fur, my thighs.
But whole years I didn't sleep beside my wife,
first for her snoring, and then for the thicket
of briar and purple thistle that grew between us,
another cat—half tabby, half Siamese, pale sky eyes—
dividing the night between our beds
while a restless creature roamed the hall.
In pet store cages guinea pigs and long-tailed rats,
ferrets, chinchillas, small white mice bred for snakes
huddle in heaps, inside their blindness,
some other sight. At night near the lake's center,
where ice thins to water cold enough to kill
me and you, geese gather, turn their long curved black necks
tailward, tuck heads between wings, folding to a pulsing core.

Two golden pumas doze on a gray stone slab
in the sun. I walk between them, humming
to spiders and millipedes I can't see,
to the great horned owl who saw me before I saw
him alone in a barren cottonwood, keeping watch.
Humming, I cross a field of frozen ash,
a roof of wind, silent paws and feet pressing
against my soles as I begin to slip,
humming to my daughter as she slips away,
as I fall through my bones, my velvet fear,
humming to myself, to no one, beside Suzanne.

Coming and Going

Some creature sunning on a boulder
seeing me
slipped so quickly down
into a black mouth
between stone and ground
I can't say what it was

⌘

A green morning in the school yard,
hole so deep I have to kneel
to peer in under the grass flap,
see the sleek brown-furred bodies
curled into themselves, a pulsing
circle of sleep, a softness held
in that pocket of earth,
and on every side the world
stretching away.

⌘

When I ask my two-year-old daughter why
she tears the summer flowers, leaving fistfuls
of tender petals—purple, canary, crimson—
she says only, "I want to get *in* them."

⌘

Death of Living Things

I lift my cat from the road and the gray snake
of her intestines slides out on the asphalt.
I almost don't recognize her,
the way the cold morning rain has matted
and stained her ginger fur a darker brown,
and her right eye so huge and round,
popped from its socket by the impact,
still staring in terror at the roaring tire,
her blood mixing with rain.

⌘

My mother zipped up in a black bag,
carried away.
I find her one night
inside her piano.

⌘

Part squirrel, part rabbit
small creatures crawl
inside our walls
I tell no one
fearing their claws and teeth
in the ducts and vents
but when I put out my hand
one by one they come
for touch, curl in my arms

⌘

Clipping my toenails on the porch
I notice a thin white crescent slowly
sliding across the bricks
then another
ants carry me away

⌘

When the leaves come back I lie beneath them,
watching the soft green arrows edge into blue,
the highways and mourning doves gathering
in the branches spreading from my chest.

Part Four

GIVING BLOOD

Between Poems

Between poems I'm a beggar
asking birds for spare seed.
I shake my tin cup: no sound.
I lift it to my ear, listen
into the hollow, hear
Rachel, four and a half, laugh
and say, "God is eating us up!"
When the ash tree in the park turns purple
I remember breathing last year
beneath its branches, how I flickered awhile
in the treetops along Prospect Street.
Now war for breakfast and dinner.
My heart is a fist that can't unclench.
Rachel decides the stars and planets
made the Earth and us. Next night,
gazing up at the glowing crescent moon
stuck to the ceiling above her bed,
she says thoughtfully, "God isn't real."
In the desert I bite through the burgundy skin
of a prickly pear: musky sweet flesh and a mouthful
of tiny seeds hard enough to crack teeth.
I spit them on the rocky earth.

PRISON POETRY

"You're not on the list," the gatekeeper said
as if he'd caught me trying to break *in*.
A large sign shouted NO CONTRABAND
but didn't include poetry
in its extended definition.
I surrendered my proof of identity,
signed a form and clipped a card to my shirt
to make "Visitor" my official name.
The inner door opened, I entered
with only words to say who I was
and why I came.

"I had trouble getting in here,"
I apologized to the waiting men,
a circle of fifteen faces, fifteen lives
numbered in blue work shirts and jeans.
"Not to worry," a voice replied.
"The hard part is getting back out."

Our laughter faded into silence.
Somewhere else, it seemed, the world went on.
We waited for something we couldn't name.
What could we say that would matter?
What could words mean in such a place?

Another voice said, "This is all
we got, right here. This is it."

We were ready to begin.

Neighbor

On the day we move into our new house
the man next door comes to welcome us
and confide he has pancreatic cancer
though he's doing well he says
he's remodeling his entire interior
and planning to join the police force
but beneath his white cowboy hat whitening hair
is failing everywhere his skin is sinking to bone
and his eyes want only to escape

No one lives with him or comes to visit
and the way he chases our cat from his porch
says maybe he's earned his loneliness by hard work
though later he says he doesn't mind the cat
and of all who live here he's the only one
who always bothers to wave or come
share some talk however small

I don't know why I'm telling you this
I'm taking up your time you have somewhere to go
and what's the point what can anyone do
anyway it happens every day
someone dies alone quietly vanishing
from a quiet street where people keep to themselves
and neighbor what does any of this
have to do with me or you

Of Unity and Wholeness

The problem with unity is the problem
with the thesis, the ego, monotheism:
Everything must fit into the Idea
or be disregarded, pushed away, driven out.
So the man came looking for his lost book,
mumbling something about quantum mechanics,
growing louder and angrier as he searched
our tables, shoving aside our books
and papers, puncturing the atmosphere
of our poetry reading, his face, hands, clothes
burnished with dirt, eyes flitting like moths
behind thick glass. When he suddenly asked
if he could take a turn at the mic, we said no.
Right about then the sun would have been rising
in Manila. An old woman I will never know,
and can say nothing more about, opened her eyes.
Every summer the fur on my cat's back
gets so matted I have to cut it off with scissors

and for many weeks after he walks around looking
like a post-op patient. Weeds grow in my garden,
even when I'm not thinking of them. Someone found
the book, *The Elegant Universe*, torn in two
unequal pieces, cover gone, outer pages
smeared and stained, pale yellow glue
splintering off the spine. The man took it
in his hands, smiled, softened. He said
his seven-year-old son had wanted to be like him,
so stole some of his stash, smoked from his hollowed
chicken-bone pipe, then ran laughing in front of a car.
One theory says a perfect, absolute unity existed
once, before creation. Since then it's all a matter
of broken symmetries. The man walked away,
out of this poem, across the street,
into the open night.

Giving Blood

Sit down between your childhood friend
dead of leukemia before he turned nine
and the drunk who shredded himself
and a family of five on the road last night.
This tan vinyl recliner has been waiting for you.
Open your best vessel. A little pain
but also popcorn, apple juice, a basketball game.
Through thin tubing the dark red flows both ways.
You're reservoir and river, a delicate cup
and what has carried the cup this far.
You're a man dying, trying to live.
You might be breathing steaming heat
in a womb of sticks and blankets,
sweat falling off your body like rain,
remembering the clouds and dirt and sun
alive in your veins, in the Methodist minister
bellowing "Blood of the Earth! Blood of the Earth!"
as you hose off his large naked body,
cock and balls bouncing as he dances
like a fool in the summer night air.
You might say, *This is not my story or my blood.*
You might say, *I can't recall where I first wet my lips.*

Albuquerque

Who are the ghosts of this grid?
Whose hunger is this, a hunger of eyes
in the endless teeth of traffic
following gleaming signs
through streets of vacant mirrors.

Whose grief keeps whispering?
Whatever we do, let's not look up
to see the storm of skulls.
Whatever we do, let's not look down
while we vomit flags and blood.

In the furnished rooms of our televisions
puppets shake our wooden hands.
Then the wind shows its throat
in the power lines, then the mountains
come walking in hats of black planets.

Sidewalk

Do you doubt I love these sidewalks,
stained and pitted as they are?
When you saw me making my daily pilgrimage
to nowhere, did you think I didn't care?
I was wondering what it means to be human.
I was asking the concrete to open its windows.
You pretended to be some harmless self, as did I,
while far away bombs screamed down in our names.
New green startled cottonwoods and elms
into flight, leaving history.
Our fingers touched a wall as we walked.
I was wondering what it means to be American.

American Marathon

We are running to catch a closing door
to escape into the future we are running
with cell phones and medicated children
because there's not enough time because
there's too much we are running running
in climate-controlled houses mounted on wheels
while the air keeps heating up forests animals
keep leaving walking the other way running
with our arms pockets storage units so full we're
stumbling running from the eyes and stomachs
of the empty-handed from blood on our shoes
from faraway places we never quite remember
with freedom profit on our lips guns in hands
God behind us world to save with our terror
our terror our innocence without pity without
mercy we are closing the door and running

The Torturer's Hands

After the dark hood stops sobbing,
stops screaming, stops breathing,
the hands go home
to lift a glass, a fork, a knife,
to stroke cat's fur, woman's skin.
Then they're put away
in the back of a drawer
where they play solitaire,
fingertips tapping a metal table,
filling with an unheard cry,
dreaming of arms.
They couldn't be your hands.
They couldn't be mine.
When the door opens and flashlights look in,
the hands are gone.

The Caskets

Please don't hide the caskets
Bring them out, remove the flags
ours and theirs, so we can try
to see each one

We need to touch the cool, smooth lids
dream of all the galaxies
plunging through the black inside

We need to carry them through the streets
a clumsy weight brought to each door
place a casket on the dinner table
a casket by the foot of the bed

Where sun strokes grasses and leaves
a gleaming casket
by the slide and the swings
in wallet, purse, pocket, grocery sack
a casket in each bite of bread

MANY KINGDOMS

Uncle Warren prayed for my pagan, pantheistic soul
to rise in the afterlife to some celestial kingdom
I never cared to imagine. When he died I saw
his hands cutting, carving, smoothing wood
into the tables, mantels, chairs and doors he gave
to everyone he liked. I didn't want to remember
how those hands shook the night he claimed al-Qaeda
was as powerful and dangerous as the Nazis,
parroting the president's recent line,
and how our dinner turned to bitterness,
Eloise finally silencing us for peace,
how we rarely spoke thereafter, divided to his end
by stupid fear and rage, the war in our blood.

Wet sand sighs with my steps. The iron breathes
through my shirt. An intermittent ticking.
Eternity is too much for the mind,
except in small doses. Who can hold his own death
in his hands, carry it through the day?

Versions of Jesus and Mohammed reach
for each other's throats.

In the grain of oak and pine: many kingdoms.

Where the Crickets Found Me

I was trying to sleep
beneath amnesiac traffic
and the clock's clubbed feet.
I was trying to breathe,
to live between the gear teeth
of an engine devouring earth and blood.
Then I heard, somewhere below,
their tiny keys opening
night's numberless doors.

Two days later in the garden,
I found beneath a large gray stone,
in a crevice between two stones below,
a single cricket, small and brownish-black.
Carefully, carefully, I put the stone back.

The Great Secret

A rattlesnake taught me to see
the holes filling this canyon
between and beneath rocks and boulders,
in the shade of chamisa and Apache plume,
in the bare desert floor: holes
that say *ant, beetle, bobcat, mountain lion.*
I walk into the mouth of the day,
feel the air open and open, taking me
in, time falling away
like a robe, leaving me naked
as the moment I opened the brown paper bag
left in the middle of a lonely road
tunneling through trees of my twelfth summer,
and found the Great Secret
in glossy pictures: bearded holes between women's legs.
I fell in, the world fell through me
and left me standing naked when my Aunt Tiger,
who knew every card game and cuss word
and could make the dead laugh,
sealed herself in her garage with her car running,
when they lowered her casket into that rectangle
cut clean in orange clay draped with fake grass.

Because I knew the smell of that clay
mixed with the smells of blood and rust
from years before when I followed my dog
back to where she'd birthed her pups
beneath an abandoned trailer, when I got down
on my stomach, stuck my head into that hole
and heard her growl at my face
in the dimness, and who was I
and who was she until she heard
my frightened, angry voice say her name?
Because in the beginning was a hole
and it made world and word to speak
into its bottomless ear, and this is the fear
and the violence of men, and why
I keep walking out, walking in.

A Peace

Maybe orange wildflowers, soft weeds
risen from your pungent wetness

or a fat lime caterpillar
rippling across the afternoon.

Where were we before we learned fear's
contagion, how it takes our measure?

Forgiven? By the dead? But then....
Love, we live with a knife, awake

inside a trembling hand, and yet
in the shadows by the back fence

the first leaves are still cool and moist
and I swear something is breathing.

Depending

Because mourning doves cooed in my head,
in rooms leafing out above.
Because I climbed a green ladder
while lying in my earthen bed.
When wind told the tree. When sky. When I turned
and drank from the well between your legs.
If we care for the calves and chicks.
If we slaughter the cows and chickens.
For the war to end. For the song to continue.
Where the window waits. While your fingers speak.

I WALK TO GET THINGS MOVING

Some robin has left his vest of rust
so recently, not even the ants have arrived
for his eyes, though the maple leaf
impression in sidewalk cement is burning
through to another green. I keep walking
and hope you'll know me when we meet.
Is the world not enough, or too much?
I touch the smooth, pencil-yellow beak,
the folded wings flying into the earth.
I want to die so I can see God
says Rachel, not yet five,
and I think of suicide bombers and Rapturists,
the urge to be done with the river,
to tear the screen, behold the Face.
Front page eyes of a young gunman
who tried to smother his own scream,
and a torturer in our mirrors.
Touch my hand, the tail-feather sheen.
New leaves, burnt walls, sky, voices of water
walk through this transparence.

Improvisation in a Changing Key

I glance up from somewhere else—
white sky streaming with birds.
The way the lake's surface doesn't stop
while the geese and ducks and breeze stay,
a moment's face kaleidoscoping
into the next, a shattering
of patterns, a forming, open-ended.
"Death is the only freedom"
the student writes at the end of his essay
in answer to the question, *Who are you?*
The dust won't glow, and now the geese
are walking and shitting on ice.
Steel and stone, help us to our hardness.
Our empty hands carry all we've lost—
this ground abides in air.
Shuffle the panes. Somewhere a dance of planes
calls for moves we've never made.

Moving

When my neighbors learned I was moving,
they invited me into their homes
for the first time, I saw their rooms,
furniture, belongings, their naked faces
as they told me their stories, I looked through
their windows at the same houses—different now—
the one I was leaving, the street.
It's because they'll never see you again
said Suzanne, and I thought of a man I'd seen,
a stranger walking with a suitcase
through some other Albuquerque street,
how he opened a hole in the air,
the habitual buildings, traffic and me
following, and now these beetle-eaten elm leaves
shedding light too wide to hold
in Reno, Nevada, the sidewalk arriving
and departing as I stand still and try
to tell a scrub jay the convoluted history
of my name, the meaning of this
scarred and bewildered face
and Galileo's last three words.
Between me and flowing water a fence,
but the children clutch a long green string
as their teacher leads them into fall,
as the house walks with time,
fire speaking in each cell,
and just a moment ago we burned
a man alive, his jaw clamped shut
in an iron mask so he wouldn't utter
again what he saw in everything, moving.